JAMES: A STUDY GUIDE
PRACTICAL WISDOM FOR
CHALLENGING TIMES

Robert Rogland

Saluda Press

Published by Saluda Press, Tacoma, WA
Printed by Gorham Printing Company, Centralia, WA.

ISBN 978-0-9965477-0-3

The Timothy Series of Bible Study Guides

James: Practical Wisdom for Challenging Times

Forthcoming:

First Corinthians: A Study Guide

Second Corinthians: A Study Guide

The Letters of Peter: Hope and Truth for Troubled Times

The Letters of John: Truth and Love

All Scripture is breathed out by God and profitable for teaching, for reproof, for correction, and for training in righteousness. *2 Timothy 3:16*

CONTENTS

ACKNOWLEDGEMENT

The author thanks members of the men's Bible study at Rose Hill Presbyterian Church, Columbia, SC, who used an earlier version of this material. Their feedback has made this study guide a better book. Any errors, irrelevance, and lack of clarity that remain are entirely my own failings.

PRACTICAL WISDOM FOR CHALLENGING TIMES

James, a brother of the Lord and the *de facto* head of the church in Jerusalem during the era of the apostles, was inspired by the Spirit of God to write a letter to "the twelve tribes in the Dispersion." His intended readers were probably Jewish Christians living in various parts of the Roman Empire and possibly the Parthian Empire as well. That letter has been recognized as part of the Holy Spirit-inspired collection of writings we call the New Testament. The Letter or Book of James is not divine history like the gospels and the Acts of the Apostles, nor does it contain much teaching falling under the heading of doctrine or theology, like the letters of the Apostle Paul. Rather, like the Book of Proverbs in the Old Testament, James is wisdom literature. James is a book of practical wisdom for Christians living in trying times.

Like believers in apostolic times, Christians today confront trials, difficulties, and temptations that call for *savoir faire* in the literal sense of that phrase: *knowing what to do*. The Book of James is God's practical word to us. The Apostle Paul tells us in Romans 12:2 to be transformed by the renewing of our minds so that we may discern the good and acceptable and perfect will of God for our lives. A study of the Book of James will help us towards that goal.

USING THIS STUDY GUIDE

Each lesson consists of a series of readings, questions, answers, and notes. The answers and notes provide answers to the questions and further remarks on the topics they raise.

Each lesson in the guide covers a natural or logical unit of James' thought. To gain a first impression of the passage, you should read the specific passage prayerfully *without reference to the Study Questions or Study Notes.* Next, read the Study Questions and study the passage looking for answers to the questions. You will grasp the contents of the passage more thoroughly by writing down the answers in a separate notebook.

After completing the Study Questions, compare your answers with those supplied in the Study Guide. Be sure to look up all the scriptural references cited in the answers. If you don't find your answers in the guide you are not necessarily off track. The questions and answers provided are meant to cover the most important points the passage has to make without implying that nothing else could be said. If you are in a class and unsure whether your answers are correct or relevant, check with the teacher and discuss your answers with other class members.

Last of all, you should read the study notes on the passage at hand. Most of the notes do not discuss individual verses or answer specific questions; rather, they deal with issues raised by the passage in whole or in part, speak to doctrinal topics, or draw implications for our faith and life. Many of the study notes go beyond the passage at hand.

The lessons have been "field tested." Based on experience, each lesson will take about a half-hour of class discussion. If the one is studying James individually, one can take as much time as needed, and a lesson can be broken up into two or more parts as desired.

Scripture quotations are taken from the English Standard Version; however, the Bible student may use any English translation with this study guide.

LESSON 1. JAMES 1:1-8

STUDY QUESTIONS

1. In v. 2 James speaks of various trials. What trials have you or people you know had to endure?

2. How have these trials tested your faith or the faith of those you know?

3. What is counter-intuitive and striking about the admonition in v. 2, "Count it all joy, my brothers, when you meet trials of various kinds"?

4. Why do suffering and trials produce two different outcomes, steadfastness in some and falling away in others?

5. What if we just don't know what to do when in the midst of trials, troubles, and suffering? *v. 5*

6. While God generously gives wisdom for living, there is a condition attached to our requests for wisdom. What is it? *vs. 6-7*

7. What if a person isn't sure that God will give the wisdom he or she needs? *vs. 7-8*

ANSWERS TO STUDY QUESTIONS

1. In v.2, James speaks of various trials. What trials have you or people you know had to endure?

Christians in America may face economic trials, such as loss of a job, failure to receive child support, credit card theft, or unexpected, overwhelming bills. Some experience difficulties in their marriages, such as infidelity, divorce or the inability to have children. Some have to deal with family problems, such as alienation from family members, an unexpected pregnancy, or rebellious children. Others may face natural disasters, like floods or hurricanes. Still others suffer from health problems, like cancer or debilitating chronic conditions. One simply cannot list all the trials Christians encounter in this vale of tears. In addition to trials common to Christians and non-Christians alike, Christians in the apostolic era faced persecution and oppression for their faith, as do Christians today in some countries.

2. How have these trials tested your faith or the faith of those you know?

Trials are a crisis of faith for many. They wonder how God could allow them to suffer such terrible trials if he is really good. Others wonder if God really loves them. Still others question whether they can really be Christians if God sends them these trials. Still others just don't know what to do or think; they are perplexed, at their wits' end, and afraid. James has answers for all of these reactions.

3. What is counter-intuitive and striking about the admonition in v. 2, "Count it all joy, my brothers, when you meet trials of various kinds"?

It is anything but natural to count it joy when we are faced with trials. Our normal reaction is to bewail them and to wish they had never come our way.

4. Why does suffering and trial produce two different outcomes, steadfastness in some and falling away in others?

Testing is a process designed to show what is genuine as well as to refine the genuine. Those who are truly born again by the Spirit of God through faith and trust in Jesus Christ are in fact those who were given to the Son of God by the Father to be his own before the foundation of the world. They are kept by the power of God. Jesus declared:

> And this is the will of him who sent me, that I should lose nothing of all that he has given me, but raise it up on the last day. *John 6:39*

And in later in John he says:

> My sheep hear my voice and I know them, and they follow me. I give them eternal life, and they will never perish, and no one will snatch them out of my hand. My father, who has given them to me, is greater than all, and no one is able to snatch them out of the Father's hand. *John 10:27-29*

5. What if we just don't know what to do when in the midst of trials, troubles, and suffering? v. 5

When we need wisdom to know what to do we should ask God for it. James assures us that God will give us all the wisdom we need. He gives generously and will not reproach us for our perplexity and ignorance.

6. While God generously gives wisdom for living, there is a condition attached to our requests for wisdom. What is it? vs. 6-7

We must ask in faith, believing that we will receive. The Christian lives by faith from beginning to end, Romans 1:17. If we are to draw near to him in prayer, asking for wisdom or any other blessing, we must draw near in faith.

7. What if a person isn't sure that God will give the wisdom he or she needs? vs. 7-8

James says that person should not expect to get anything from the Lord. The author of the Book of Hebrews affirms the same:

> And without faith it is impossible to please him, for whoever would draw near to God must believe that he exists and that he rewards those who seek him. *Hebrews 11:6*

Though neither James nor the author of Hebrews says so, experience shows that people who doubt that God will actually make us a plain way through the wilderness are likely to disregard any wisdom God gives - it is easy to think of it as just one other idea that probably won't work.

James calls such people *doubleminded*. He uses the word *doubleminded* again in 4:8. There it refers not to a doubter, but to one who tries to love both God and the world. Such a person is indeed doubleminded, though not in the same sense as the person in 1:6-8.[1] We'll expand on that in Lesson

---

[1] The same Greek word is found in both 1:8 and 4:8, and the ESV translators rendered it *doubleminded* in both passages. Greek words, like English words, sometimes have distinctly different meanings

STUDY NOTES

1. Who was James?

"James, a servant of God and of the Lord Jesus Christ" is almost certainly James the brother of the Lord. The New Testament mentions as least three men named James who were part of the apostolic circle: James the son of Zebedee, James the son of Alphaeus, and James the brother of the Lord.

The author of this letter cannot be James the son of Zebedee, one of the original twelve apostles, for he was executed early on by King Herod, Acts 12:1-2, 17. The New Testament tells us nothing about James the son of Alphaeus after Pentecost. But we find that James the brother of the Lord, while not one of the original apostles (indeed, he did not believe in Jesus until he rose from the dead), was considered to be a "pillar" of the church, Galatians 2:9. An indication of his importance in the early church is that he presided over the first all-church council, the Council of Jerusalem, Acts 2:17-25; 15:12-13 ff.

James acknowledged a special, personal obligation towards Jewish Christians. When Paul and Barnabas came to Jerusalem to meet with James, Cephas (Peter), and John, the men came to an agreement. Paul and Barnabas would focus on evangelizing the Gentiles while Peter, James, and John would focus on evangelizing the Jews, Galatians 2:9. This letter, addressed to Jewish Christians, "the twelve tribes of the Dispersion," is a manifestation of the pastoral responsibility James felt for his Jewish Christian brothers and sisters.

All the evidence we have, while not conclusive, strongly suggests that it was James the Lord's brother who wrote this letter.

2. Why do we have testing and trials?

James tells his readers to rejoice because trials result in a good end for God's children. Testing produces steadfastness, endurance, and patience under trial, and steadfastness builds Christian character. So, he says, continue to bear up and let steadfastness mold you into a mature, "perfect" Christian.

The Apostle Paul taught exactly the same thing:

> ...we rejoice in our suffering, knowing that suffering produces endurance, and endurance produces character, and character produces hope. And hope does not put us to shame, because God's love has been poured into our hearts through the Holy Spirit who has been given to us. *Romans 5:3-5*

Peter also makes the point:

> In this you rejoice, though now for a little while, if necessary, you have been grieved by various trials, so that the tested genuineness of your faith - more precious than gold that perishes though it is tested by fire - may be found to result in praise and glory and honor at the revelation of Jesus Christ. *1 Peter 1:6-7*

3. Why do some pass the test and some fail?

Suffering and trial do not produce endurance in everyone. Consider the Lord's words in the parable of the four kinds of ground:

Other seeds fell on rocky ground, where they did not have much soil, and immediately they sprang up, since they had no depth of soil, but when the sun rose they were scorched. And since they had no root, they withered away.

As for what was sown on rocky ground, this is the one who hears the word and immediately receives it with joy, yet has no root in himself, but endures for a while, and when tribulation or persecution arises on account of the word, immediately falls away. *Matthew 13:5-6, 20-21*

James doesn't get into the theology of why the elect (those chosen by God to be a people for his Son) are preserved; he simply asserts that trials and sufferings will produce mature Christian character. It is clear that he has genuine Christians in mind, those born again of imperishable seed, 1 Peter 1:23.

It's worth observing at this point that testing and trial often are occasions of temptation. (The Greek word for *testing* also means *temptation*; it is the context that indicates which meaning is in view. We will consider temptation in Lesson 2.) With temptation, as with testing, God provides wisdom as to what to do - in the case of temptation, wisdom to escape it. We have the promise in 1 Corinthians 10:13:

No temptation has overtaken you that is not common to man. God is faithful, and he will not let you be tempted beyond your ability, but with the temptation he will also provide the way of escape, that you may be able to endure it.

LESSON 2. JAMES 1:9-15

STUDY QUESTIONS

1. In v. 12 James speaks of the lowly brother and (especially) of the rich brother. How are his admonitions related to the matter of testing and trial?

2. What is the exaltation the poor man should rejoice in? *v. 9*

3. What is the humiliation the rich man should rejoice in? *v. 9*

4. Besides wealth and poverty, what other situations in life can be sources of testing and temptation?

5. What is the true source of temptation? *v. 14*

6. What is the difference between *testing* and *temptation* as regards: (a) the source, and (b) the results? *vs. 14-15*

ANSWERS TO STUDY QUESTIONS

1. In 1:12 James speaks of the lowly brother and (especially) of the rich brother. How are his admonitions related to the matter of testing and trial?

Both poverty and riches test a person. The poor are more likely to be oppressed than the rich (2:6-7). They may be tempted to steal, or to despair and think God doesn't care about them. The rich may be tempted to use their money and power to oppress and defraud the poor, or to abandon their dependence on God and think they have achieved wealth and success through brains, hard work, and thrift.

2. What is the exaltation the poor man should rejoice in? v. 9

The believing poor are "rich in faith and heirs of the kingdom, which [God] has promised to those who love him," 2:5. Paul spells it out in Ephesians 1:3, 18-19.

> God…has blessed us in Christ with every spiritual blessing in the heavenly places.

> …that you may know what is the hope to which he has called you, what are the riches of his glorious inheritance in the saints, and what is the immeasurable greatness of his power toward us who believe….

3. What is the humiliation the rich man should rejoice in? v. 9

He should rejoice, first, in the certain knowledge that his riches will fade away, often "in the midst of his pursuits." Jesus told the parable of the rich man and his barns to make the very point that a rich man, like all men, needs to get right with God more than he needs to safeguard his worldly possessions. Riches are a great temptation to self-satisfaction. Trusting in them rather than Christ leaves one utterly unprepared when God calls one to judgment, Luke 12:16-21. A rich man needs to become poor in spirit if he is to see his need of Christ, repent, and cast himself on Christ for his salvation, and so inherit the kingdom of heaven, Matthew 5:3.

4. Besides wealth and poverty, what other situations in life can be sources of testing and temptation?

See the answer to Study Question 1, Lesson 1.

5. What is the true source of temptation? v. 14

The true source of temptation is our own desire. We may blame Satan, but Satan cannot tempt us to do anything we don't want to do. A straight, heterosexual man will not be tempted by another man, no matter how handsome, since he has no sexual desire for men; a child stuffed with dessert will not be tempted to take cake from the plate of the child next to him, since he has no desire for any more sweets.

Consider Eve: She would not have been tempted by Satan's words alone if they had not spoken to her desires:

> So when the woman saw that the tree was good for food, and that it was a delight to the eyes, and that the tree was to be desired to make one

14

wise, she took of its fruit and ate, and she also gave some to her husband who was with her, and he ate. *Genesis 3:6*

The Apostle John agrees with James that the source of temptations is not God, but our own desires:

For all that is in the world—the desires of the flesh and the desires of the eyes and the pride of life—is not from the Father but is from the world. *1 John 2:16-17*

Some desires are not bad in themselves, but if fixed on a forbidden object they can still lead to sin. And as James tells us, sin leads to death. Paul said the same thing in Romans 6:16 and 23:

You are the slaves of the one whom you obey, either of sin, which leads to death, or of obedience, which leads to righteousness.

For the wages of sin is death, but the free gift of God is eternal life in Christ Jesus our Lord.

5. What is the difference between testing and temptation as regards: (a) the source, and (b) the results? vs. 14-15

a. The source of testing is God; the source of temptation is our own desire.

b. The results of testing and trial for the Christian are steadfastness, which produces mature Christian character, and, ultimately, the crown of life, v. 13.

STUDY NOTES

1. More on testing and temptation.

In James 1:1-8 (Lesson 1) we found that James tells us to count it all joy when we fall into various trials and difficulties because they produce steadfastness (or endurance), and steadfastness matures us and perfects our character. If we lack wisdom to know what to do under trial we are to ask it of God, who will give us freely and generously the wisdom we need. But we must ask in faith; if we doubt that he will give us wisdom, he will not.

In verses 9-15 James continues his remarks on testing, and also discusses temptation, which often stems from testing and trial.

2. The lowly and the mighty.

James's remarks to the lowly and the wealthy bring to mind Mary's inspired words upon hearing that she would be the mother of the Savior:

> [God] has shown strength with his arm; he has scattered the proud in the thoughts of their hearts; he has brought down the mighty from their thrones and exalted those of humble estate; he has filled the hungry with good things, and the rich he has sent away empty. *Luke 1:51-58*

3. Peirasmos, an ambiguous Greek word.

In 1:9-15 James returns to the matter of steadfastness and endurance, and he introduces a new wrinkle: temptation. James's original readers may have been prone to identify testing with temptation, not only because testing, trials, and difficulties are often occasions of temptation, but also because *testing* and *temptation* were both denoted by the same Greek word, *peirasmos*. The reader had to decide which meaning the word had from the context. That may not always have been clear.

3. Sin leads to death.

James makes it clear that sin leads to death. This truth is found throughout the Bible. But is he warning *Christians* that they can lose their salvation if they fall into persistent, unrepented sin? Didn't Jesus promise that not one of his own will be lost?

We should view James's words of warning as intended for (a) readers who think themselves Christians but have not a living faith in Christ, that is, those who have not been born again, and also as intended for (b) true Christians, to prevent them from giving themselves over to sin.

a. From its earliest days the church has had weeds among the wheat, the unsaved among the saved, Matthew 13:24-30 and 36-43; see Acts 5:1-11 and 8:9-24 for early instances. James warns them in the hope that they will recognize the danger of their sinful desires and ways, repent, and cast themselves on Christ for salvation.

b. If a born-again person follows his or her sinful desires into actual persistent sinful conduct, he or she *will* die. But James's warning is meant to prevent that, and it will prevent it for those who belong to Christ. Some scriptural warnings or predictions are hypothetical. Jonah flatly predicted that God would overthrow Nineveh in forty days, but Nineveh repented and was spared. The warning was hypothetical.

LESSON 3. JAMES 1:16-27

STUDY QUESTIONS

1. How might we be deceived regarding the good things that come our way? *v. 16*

2. James refers to God as the "Father of lights," v. 17. That's an odd term, used nowhere else in the Bible. What do you suppose it means?

3. The lights of heaven are good gifts, but God is better. What shows him to be better? *v. 17*

4. What is the greatest proof that God has good will towards us, that he wills to do us good and give us good gifts? *v. 18*

5. What is the general subject of vs. 19-27?

6. Verses 19-21 contain four imperatives or commands. What are they?

7. What does it mean to be a doer of the Word? *v. 22*

8. In v. 25 James refers to the "law of liberty." What is this law of liberty?

9. Of what does pure and undefiled religion consist? *v. 27*

ANSWERS TO STUDY QUESTIONS

1. How might we be deceived regarding the good things that come our way? v. 16

Our sinful human nature is prone either to chalk our blessings up to our own intelligence, skill, and effort, or else to conclude that we were just lucky. God warned his ancient people Israel against such thinking:

> Take care lest you forget the LORD your God...lest, when you have eaten and are full and have built good houses and live in them, and when your herds and flocks multiply and your silver and gold is multiplied and all that you have is multiplied, then your heart be lifted up, and you forget the LORD your God, who brought you out of the land of Egypt, out of the house of slavery...who fed you in the wilderness....Beware lest you say in your heart, "My power and the might of my hand have gotten me this wealth." *Deuteronomy 8:11-18*

2. James refers to God as the "Father of lights," v. 17. That's an odd term, used nowhere else in the Bible. What do you suppose it means?

At least three meanings are possible:

a. James may simply be reminding his readers that "God is light, and in him is no darkness at all," 1 John 1:5. While we must not forget this, it does not seem to relate to the rest of the paragraph and is unlikely to be what James has in mind.

b. Sinclair Ferguson suggests another meaning in his book, *In Christ Alone: Living the Gospel Centered Life*:

> God's sovereign action in Creation serves as a model for His equally sovereign action in our spiritual re-creation. Paul never ceases to be amazed that the same God who said, "'Let light shine out of darkness,' made his light shine in our hearts to give us the light of the knowledge of the glory of God in the face of Christ," *2 Corinthians 4.6, NIV*

James may be affirming along with Paul that the God who created the lights of heaven has given us the light of the gospel so that, just as the sun causes the earth to bring forth vegetation, so the word of truth brings forth a new humanity from the mass of men and women dead in sin, v. 18.

c. A third possible meaning is suggested by James's main point in these verses. God is the author of *all* good gifts. James may be citing the lights of heaven as one of God's greatest gifts to all humankind, believers and unbelievers. Genesis 1:14-19 recounts the creation of the sun, moon, and stars. The account of the fourth day of creation concludes by stating that God declared this work good, Genesis 1:14. The Lord Jesus made this point by reminding us that God sends life-giving rain on the unjust as well as the just, Matthew 5:45.

3. The lights of heaven are good gifts, but God is better. What shows him to be better? (v. 17)

The lights of heaven change with time. As the moon goes through its monthly cycle it varies, waxing and waning; as sun and moon daily move across the sky, shadows change, v. 17. But God never changes. We can depend on him to keep his promises; we can rest on his unchanging grace and mercy.

> For I the LORD do not change; therefore you, O children of Jacob, are not consumed. *Malachi 3:6*

> Jesus Christ is the same yesterday and today and forever. *Hebrews 13:8*

Thomas Chisholm clearly had James's words in mind when he penned the words of the popular hymn, *Great is Thy Faithfulness:*

> Great is thy faithfulness, O God my Father;
> There is no shadow of turning with Thee,
> Thou changest not, Thy compassions they fail not,
> As Thou hast been, Thou forever wilt be.

We must bear this in mind or we will be *doubleminded* when we pray; see the answer to question 1 in Lesson 1.

4. What is the greatest proof that God has good will towards us, that he wills to do us good and give us good gifts? v. 18

God gave us a new birth "of his own will." He was under no necessity to do so. And he used the Word to bring about that new birth. Just as the light of the sun gives new life to the earth every spring, so we are born again through the light of the Word. As Peter wrote,

You have been born again, not of perishable seed but of imperishable, through the living and abiding word of God. *1 Peter 1:23*

5. What is the general subject of vs. 19-27?

James turns to a new subject in these verses, urging us to be doers of the word and not hearer only. In 1:18 he said that God "brought us forth by the word of truth." But hearing the word does not automatically save. Many hear the word of truth and are not brought forth into new life. James warns us against deceiving ourselves, 1:22. We must *receive* that word and take it into our hearts in faith, as he says in 1:21: "receive...the implanted word which is able to save your souls." Verses 19-27 unpack these ideas.

6. Verses 19-21 contain four imperatives or commands. What are they?

a. Be quick to listen and learn.

b. Be slow to speak.

In commanding these things the Book of James stands with the other wisdom literature of the Bible, in particular, the Book of Proverbs:

The wise of heart will receive commandments, but a babbling fool will come to ruin. *Proverbs 10:8*

The wise lay up knowledge, but the mouth of a fool brings ruin near. *Proverbs 10:14*

When words are many, transgression is not lacking, but whoever restrains his lips is prudent. *Proverbs 10:19*

James amplifies this point in v. 26.

c. Be slow to anger. We deceive ourselves when we think that we are right with God simply because we get angry with sin in others. Too often what we consider righteous wrath is nothing more than anger proceeding from our sinful nature. Even the godliest people have fallen into sin when they let their anger control them. A prime example is Moses, who struck the rock in the desert at Meribah when provoked by the complaints and unbelief of the Israelites, Numbers 20:10-13.

d. Meekly repent, that is, put away our sin, and believe, that is, receive the word of truth regarding the way of salvation.

7. What does it mean to be a doer of the Word? v. 22

a. First, it means to see ourselves in the Word for what we really are, sinners in need of a Savior, vs. 22-23.

b. Secondly, it means to repent of our sins, that is, to grieve over them and turn from them, v. 21a.

c. Thirdly, it means to receive the Word in meekness and faith, v. 21.

8. In v. 25 James refers to the "law of liberty." What is this law of liberty?

The law of liberty is the rule of life for those who have been set free from sin and from the law of God as a means of attaining righteousness with God.

> But thanks be to God, that you who were once slaves of sin have become obedient from the heart to the standard of teaching to which you

were committed, and having been set free from sin, have become slaves of righteousness. *Romans 6:17-18*

But now we are released from the law, having died to that which held us captive, so that we serve in the new way of the Spirit and not in the old way of the written code. *Romans 7:6*

For the law of the Spirit of life has set you free in Christ Jesus from the law of sin and death. *Romans 8:2*

For if you live according to the flesh you will die, but if by the Spirit you put to death the deeds of the body, you will live. For all who are led by the Spirit of God are sons of God. Romans *8:13-14*

9. Of what does pure and undefiled religion consist? v. 27

James mentions visiting widows and orphans in their affliction and keeping oneself unspotted from the world. We should consider visiting widows and orphans as representative acts of Christian love, not as our whole duty. There are the sick and prisoners to visit, the naked to clothe, and the hungry to feed, among others who need our help. See Matthew 25:31-40.

STUDY NOTES

1. Two new topics.

James dealt with trials and temptations in 1:3-15. The rest of chapter 1 deals with two new topics. Verses 16-18 are a reminder that every good gift is from God, and vs. 19-27 urge the doing of the word and not the hearing only.

James begins each of these new subjects by addressing his hearers or readers as "my beloved brothers." James often (though not always) begins a new section with "my beloved brothers," "my brothers," or simply "brothers." The ESV translation points out in a footnote that the Greek word rendered *brothers* can mean siblings of both sexes. What James has to say is for all Christians, male and female.

2. The "first fruits" of his creatures, v. 18.

James says we are a "first fruits" of his creatures, that is, of his new creation. By *we* he probably means himself and his original readers, the first believers of the apostolic period. You and I, some two thousand years later, are not the first fruits, but rather part of the great harvest that came after.

3. Being a doer of the Word: What it does not mean.

Being a doer of the Word does *not* mean that we are to do the good works the law of God requires in the expectation or hope that we will be good enough to earn God's saving approval. The Apostle Paul is the great exponent of the truth that we are saved by grace through faith and not by works. James, who gives us wisdom for living, does not repeat that gospel truth here. He does take up the question of faith and works in chapter 2. See Lesson 5.

4. Do Christians live under law?

Christians are not "under the law" as a means of being justified at God's judgment seat on the Day of Judgment, but they are under the "law of liberty," a law appropriate to a liberated people as a rule of life. A free people is not without law. Americans prize their freedom, but they know they must live under law - not the kind of law people live under in a totalitarian or dictatorial regime, but law appropriate to a free people. So we Christians live under the law of Christ, Galatians 6:2, or the law of the Spirit of life, Romans 8:2. James has more to say about the law of liberty in chapter 2 (see 2:12), where he also calls it the "royal law," 2:8. We will learn more about it there.

5. Talking the talk vs. walking the walk.

In vs. 26-27 James returns to the subject of taming the tongue, first mentioned in v. 19. He contrasts a religion of big talk with religion that is "pure and undefiled before God" in v. 27. The Greek word *threskeia*, which English versions translate *religion* here, more often than not refers to religious *service*, what the worshiper *does* to serve God, rather than one's creed or code of beliefs. The emphasis on what one does rather than what one believes is consistent with James's preoccupation with practical Christian living; it is also consistent with his exhortations to not deceive oneself. Too many who name the name of Christ do deceive themselves. They can talk the talk of evangelical religion, so they think they are Christians. But they fail to live as Christ commanded, loving their neighbor as themselves. As Jesus said, "You will recognize them by their fruits," Matthew 7:16. We need to ask ourselves if we are simply all talk, or if we live out our faith, as James urges.

LESSON 4. JAMES 2:1-13

STUDY QUESTIONS

1. Why is partiality inconsistent with the faith of Jesus Christ? *v.5*

2. Read 1 Corinthians 1:26-29. Is it really true that God shows no favoritism? Do these verses in 1 Corinthians suggest that God actually favors the poor, the have-nots, and the nobodies over the rich, important, and intellectual people?

3. Is it wrong to love and favor our own children more than other children? Is it wrong to love our fellow Christians more than unbelievers?

4. What external factors might move you or your church to partiality? Whom might you favor? Whom might you look down on?

5. "You shall love your neighbor as yourself" is called the "royal law" in v. 8. Why?

6. We saw earlier that partiality is inconsistent with the gospel of Christ. In v. 9 we see that it is also a *sin*. What makes it a sin?

7. Why is partiality a serious sin?

8. What is the "law of liberty," 2:12, also 1:25? Is it the same as the "royal law?"

ANSWERS TO STUDY QUESTIONS

1. Why is partiality inconsistent with the faith of Jesus Christ? v.5

It is inconsistent with the Christian faith because God shows no partiality:

> God shows no partiality. *Romans 2:11*

2. Read 1 Corinthians 1:26-29. Is it really true that God shows no favoritism? Do these verses suggest that God actually favors the poor, the have-nots, and the nobodies over the rich, important, and intellectual people?

Look for the reasons given in the 1 Corinthians passage for God's choice of the lowly. He chose those who were not wise, not powerful, and not of noble birth in order to shame the wise, the powerful, and the noble, so that no one should glory in his presence. In short, he chose whom he chose for his own glory.

To be sure, it is also true that God chose his elect out of love:

> The LORD your God has chosen you to be a people for his treasured possession, out of all the peoples who are on the face of the earth. It was not because you were more in number than any other people that the LORD set his love on you and chose you, for you were the fewest of all peoples, but it is because the LORD loves you. *Deuteronomy 7:6-8.*

We cannot probe into the whys and wherefores of God's love; it is unfathomable. God's acting for his own glory and acting out of love are intertwined in a way that we cannot understand.

We can only praise the glory of his grace and thank him for the love that sent Jesus to the cross.

3. Is it wrong to love and favor our own children more than other children? Is it wrong to love our fellow Christians more than unbelievers?

No, these things are not wrong. Jesus himself loved John more than the other disciples, John 13:23. The particular case of partiality that James condemns shows us the kind of partiality or favoritism we are to shun. We are to reject any favoritism based on external factors.

4. What external factors might move you or your church to partiality? Whom might you favor? Whom might you look down on?

Perhaps you or your church family would tend to look more favorably on visitors who look middle-class like you. If you are slim you may look down on the obese. According to most African-Americans, racism is still a source of partiality in our nation. You can think of other factors that incline us to be partial. We would do well to examine ourselves for favoritism based on externals, whether in thought or in deed.

5. "You shall love your neighbor as yourself" is called the "royal law" in v. 8. Why?

Two possible reasons present themselves:

a. Jesus, the Lord of glory (2:1) and our king, affirmed it as one of the two great commandments:

A lawyer asked him a question…."Teacher, which is the great commandment in the Law?" And he said to him, "You shall love the Lord your God with all your heart and with all your soul and with all your mind. This is the great and first commandment. And a second is like it: You shall love your neighbor as yourself. On these two commandments depend all the Law and the Prophets. *Matthew 22:35-40*

b. It sums up and governs the doing of the other commandments; it is royal because it rules them.

How is this so?

Except for the fourth and fifth commandments, the Ten Commandments are worded negatively. But there is a positive side to the negatively worded commandments. (Questions 44-81 of the Westminster Shorter Catechism expound the meaning of the Ten Commandments in both their negative and positive aspects.) "You shall not murder" tells us what not to do. But loving our neighbor gives the commandment a positive side. We are to do all we can to preserve our neighbor's life and health. "You shall not bear false witness" tells us what not to say about our neighbor. But if we love our neighbor we will do all we can to speak well of him and maintain his good name and reputation. Merely not stealing does not show love for our neighbor; doing what is in our power to foster his material well-being is what shows love. It is the same with the other commandments. Love governs how we carry them out.

6. We saw earlier that partiality is inconsistent with the gospel of Christ. In v. 9 we see that it is also a sin. What makes it a sin?

It is a sin because we do not love our neighbor as ourselves if we show partiality.

7. Why is partiality a serious sin?

James tells us that to break one point of the law is to break the whole law, v. 16.

8. What is the "law of liberty," 2:12, also 1:25? Is it the same as the "royal law?"

The "law of liberty" is the "law of the Spirit of life," Romans 8:2. It is the law of God and it is the royal law, but as lived out by those who have been liberated from sin and death by Christ.

> Jesus said to the Jews who had believed him, "If you abide in my word, you are truly my disciples, and you will know the truth and the truth will set you free." They answered him, "We are offspring of Abraham and have never been enslaved to anyone. How is it that you say, 'you will become free'?" Jesus answered them, "Truly, truly, I say to you, everyone who practices sin is a slave to sin. The slave does not remain in the house forever; the son remains forever. So if the Son sets you free, you will be free indeed. *John 8:31-36*

> But now we are released from the law, having died to that which held us captive, so that we serve in the new way of the Spirit and not in the old way of the written code. *Romans 7:6*

> The law of the Spirit of life has set you free in Christ Jesus from the law of sin and death. For

God has done what the law, weakened by the flesh, could not do. By sending his own Son in the likeness of sinful flesh and for sin, he condemned sin in the flesh, in order that the righteous requirement of the law might be fulfilled in us, who walk not according to the flesh but according to the Spirit. *Romans 8:2-4*

We have been freed from the law as a master that must be obeyed upon pain of death; we now serve freely and willingly as we are led by the Spirit of life.

STUDY NOTES

1. Review of chapter 1.

In 1:16-27 James reminded us that every good gift is from God. He also stressed that we need to do more than simply listen to the Word of God; we need to obey it, to do it. His emphasis was another example of the practical nature of James's letter. God inspired other New Testament authors to expound the great, precious truths of redemption; he inspired James to write about *praxis*, the practice of our faith.

In chapter 2 James seeks to correct his readers' *praxis* in the matter of showing partiality. He asserts that they are not doers of the Word when they show favoritism based on external differences.

2. Partiality.

The Jews thought God was partial to them and would show them favoritism in the final judgment, but they were wrong. All men will be judged by the same law of God, whether written by the finger of God on stone tablets for the Jews or written by God on the heart of Jews and Gentiles alike.

> For God shows no partiality. For all who have sinned without the law will also perish without the aw, and all who have sinned under the law will be judged by the law....For when Gentiles, who do not have the law, by nature do what the law requires, they are a law to themselves even though they do not have the law. They show that the work of the law is written on their hearts.... *Romans 2:11-12, 14-15*

Moreover, all who are saved are saved by the same Jesus Christ through the same faith in him. God does not have one way of salvation for some and another way for his favorites.

> Is God the God of Jews only? Is he not the God of Gentiles also? Yes, of Gentiles also, since God is one - who will justify the circumcised by faith and the uncircumcised through faith. *Romans 3:29-3*

We shall see in 2:9 that showing partiality or favoritism is not merely inconsistent with the Christian faith; it is a sin which makes one a breaker of the whole law of God.

3. Judged under the law of liberty

The New Testament clearly teaches that Christians will stand before the judgment seat of Christ like other men and women. It teaches that all will be judged according to their works, Romans 2:5-16, 2 Corinthians 5:10, Revelation 20:12-15. If that were the whole story, we should all cower in fear of judgment, for by works of the law shall no one be justified, Romans 3:20. But James says that those who know Christ will be judged under the law of liberty, 2:12. What does that mean?

In brief, it means that we who are Christ's have been set free from the law, that is, the Law of Moses, Galatians 5:1, 13-14, and are now under the law of Christ. That law is summed up in one word: love

> For you were called to freedom, brothers. Only do not use your freedom as an opportunity for the flesh, but through love serve one another.

For the whole law is fulfilled in one word: "You shall love your neighbor as yourself." *Galatians 5:13-14*.

The law of liberty, then, is the law of love, the code of conduct for a people freed by Christ from the law of sin and death. To be sure, love is a motivation and not a prescription. The biblical commandments prescribe what we should do and not do; love shows us how to do them, and in so doing it shows us their full scope. For example, it is one thing not to murder. I have never wanted to kill my neighbor. But my restraint doesn't require love, merely self-control and the absence of means, motive, and opportunity. Love on the other hand moves me to do everything in my power to preserve my neighbor's life and health.

We will be judged by this law in two ways:

a. Our works will serve to show whether we belong to Christ or not. Our conduct will not earn us a place in Christ's kingdom, but it will show if we belong there. As James writes in the following section, our works show our faith, 2:14-26. That is the subject of Lesson 5.

b. Our works also determine our heavenly reward, 1 Corinthians 3:10-15.

LESSON 5. JAMES 2:14-26

STUDY QUESTIONS

1. People with a certain kind of faith deceive themselves. What kind of faith is that? *v. 14*

2. What is the nature of the works described in vs. 13-15? Are they works of mercy? Personal works of holiness? Some other kind of works?

3. Describe dead faith - what does it look like?

4. Why does James cite the examples of Abraham and Rahab from the Old Testament? *vs. 21-25*

5. We see that a living faith expresses itself in appropriate action. What would be appropriate action for someone who believes the following?

　　a. "everyone who calls on the name of the Lord shall be saved." *Acts 2:21.*

　　b. "the prayer of faith will save the one who is sick, and the Lord will raise him up." *James 5:15.*

　　c. "One gives freely, yet grows all the richer; another withholds what he should give, and only suffers want." *Proverbs 11:24.*

ANSWERS TO STUDY QUESTIONS

1. People with a certain kind of faith deceive themselves. What kind of faith is that? v. 14

It is a faith unaccompanied by works, a faith "by itself." It corresponds to hearing the Word and agreeing with it without doing it, which James warned against in chapter 1.

2. What is the nature of the works described in vs. 13-15? Are they works of mercy? Personal works of holiness? Some other kind of works?

Clothing the ill-clad and feeding the hungry are certainly works of mercy. But we will see that the works James says are necessary include other actions that cannot be described as works of mercy - the action of Abraham in vs. 21-23 was not an act of mercy, not a "good work" in the normal sense of that term. *The works James has in mind are those that show one's faith to be real.* If a person believes A, he must do B. If he does not do B, he really does not believe A; his faith is a dead faith

3. Describe dead faith - what does it look like?

It is an abstract faith, mental and verbal only. For example, when asked, "Are you a sinner?" someone may answer, "Sure I'm a sinner, nobody's perfect." But if that person has no sorrow for his sin, no fear of God's judgment, if he has not cast himself on Christ for salvation, then his faith is dead. Again, someone may be asked, "Who is Jesus Christ?" and may answer, "Jesus is the Son of God and the Savior." But if he does not bow before Jesus Christ as *his* God and does not ask him to be *his* Savior, his faith is

41

a dead, useless faith. He believes that Jesus is the Son of God in the same way he believes Paris is the capital of France: both are equally insignificant to his life.

4. Why does James cite the examples of Abraham and Rahab from the Old Testament? vs. 21-25

He wants to illustrate the truth that faith requires appropriate works to be a living faith. His Jewish audience would consider examples from Israel's history to be evidence.

5. We see that a living faith expresses itself in appropriate action. What would be appropriate action for someone who believes the following?

a. "everyone who calls on the name of the Lord shall be saved," Acts 2:21.

He or she will call on the Lord for salvation.

b. "the prayer of faith will save the one who is sick, and the Lord will raise him up," James 5:15.

The sick person, or his friends, will pray to God for healing.

c. "One gives freely, yet grows all the richer; another withholds what he should give, and only suffers want," Proverbs 11:24.

He or she will be generous, not holding on to every penny.

STUDY NOTES

1. Ways we deceive ourselves.

James 2:14-26 introduces a new topic. We see this not only from the change of subject matter, but also from the tell-tale address, "my brothers," which usually indicates another subject.

Three times earlier in the letter James warned his readers against self-deceit:

a. In 1:16-18 he told them not to be deceived into thinking that any good gift they receive comes from anything or anyone other than God.

b. In 1:22-25 he told them not to deceive themselves by thinking that simply hearing the preaching of the Word is sufficient for a Christian. They must be doers of the Word, acting on its commandments.

c. In 1:26-27 he told them they deceive themselves if they think talking a good game makes them Christians even though they don't practice mercy and live holy lives.

In the passage before us James again warns against deceiving ourselves, though he doesn't use the word *deceive*. Here he warns against thinking that faith without works can save. We will want to see what he means by *faith* and what he means by *works* as we study this passage.

2. "Let's eat grandma" vs. "Let's eat, grandma." Punctuation matters.

The punctuation in the ESV makes v. 18 confusing. We should remember that the original Greek of the Book of James had no punctuation at all; all punctuation has been introduced by the

43

translators. I don't think James is introducing an imaginary debater, "someone" who says he doesn't need faith because he has works, as the clause, "But someone will say, 'You have faith and I have works,'" suggests. If we move the closing quotation mark to the end of v. 18 and think of the whole verse as the argument of "someone" *agreeing* with James, the verse makes more sense. Verse 18 would then read,

> But someone will say, "You have faith and I have works. Show me your faith apart from your works and I will show you my faith by my works."

The "someone" is an ally of James, challenging the "faith alone" person to give some sort of evidence that his faith is real; the "someone" has works which are evidence of his faith.

3. Faith that does not save.

When we remember that James was writing to "the twelve tribes in the Dispersion," that is, to Jewish Christians, we can appreciate his warning to those who believed that God is one, that is, that there is only one God. The Jews were the *only* monotheists, believers in one God only, in the Greco-Roman world. The pagans all around them were polytheists, believers in many gods. James may have surmised that some of his readers were unconverted Jews who admired Jesus but smugly felt that faith in one God was all they needed to get them in God's good graces. He sets them straight: such a faith can be as dead as the faith of their pagan neighbors.

44

4. Abraham's living faith.

Read Genesis 22:1-19.

The story of Abraham's life furnishes several examples of Abraham's faith, but the high point of his life of faith is his response to God's command to sacrifice his son Isaac, the son of promise, on Mount Moriah. The author of the Book of Hebrews describes Abraham's obedience of faith:

> By faith Abraham, when he was tested, offered up Isaac, and he who had received the promises was in the act of offering up his only son, of whom it was said, "Through Isaac shall your offspring be named." He considered that God was able even to raise him from the dead, from which, figuratively speaking, he did receive him back. *Hebrews 11:17-19*

If Abraham had claimed to believe God's promise that Isaac would be his heir but had refused to sacrifice him, it would have shown his faith to be dead. As it was, his works validated his faith. Indeed, Abraham's testing perfected his faith, just as James described back in 1:2-3.

5. Rahab's living faith.

Read Joshua 2:1-21 and 6:22-25.

Rahab was a Canaanite prostitute who lived in the city of Jericho. When the Israelites were about to cross the Jordan River and invade Canaan, they sent spies to reconnoiter the land. Rahab took them in and hid them from her own countrymen, who were searching for them. In Joshua 2:11-12 we read her confession of faith:

45

The LORD your God, he is God in the heavens above and on the earth beneath. Now then, please swear to me by the LORD that, as I have dealt kindly with you, you also will deal kindly with my father's house....

Rahab had come to believe that the LORD was the only God; she believed that he would give her city over to the Israelites. But she also believed that he would incline the hearts of the Israelites to show her mercy if she showed mercy to the spies. The author of the Book of Hebrews sums up her faith in Hebrews 11:31:

Rahab the prostitute did not perish with those who were disobedient, because she had given a friendly welcome to the spies.

If her faith had been a mere intellectual thing, a dead thing, she would have huddled terrified in her house until the walls of Jericho came tumbling down and she and her family had perished. But her faith was a living faith, which expressed itself in action to the salvation of herself and her family. She was rewarded not only with life: she became an ancestor of Jesus Christ, Matthew 1:5.

LESSON 6. JAMES 3:1-18

STUDY QUESTIONS

1. Why should few seek to be teachers? *vs. 1-2*

2. In what ways may a teacher stumble? *v. 2*

3. James asserts that we all stumble in many ways, especially in our speech. List some ways we stumble and sin in our speech.

4. What is James's point in vs. 4-5, where he uses horses and ships as examples?

5. What is James's main point in vs. 5-10?

6. What is the over-all theme of these verses?

7. How does one (in particular, a teacher, preacher, or corrector of morals) show himself to be wise? *v. 13*

8. What does *meekness* mean in the Bible, vs. 13-14? Helpful hint: look for the opposite of meekness in these verses; that will help you know what the biblical idea of meekness is.

9. Apparently some of those James had in mind boasted about being wise but were not. What showed their so-called wisdom to be unspiritual, earthly, from the devil? *v. 16*

10. In contrast to unspiritual, devilish "wisdom," what are the hallmarks of divine wisdom from above? *v. 17*

11. What are the results of wisdom sown (that is, taught or shared) in peace? *v. 18*

ANSWERS TO STUDY QUESTIONS

1. Why should few seek to be teachers? vs. 1-2

Those who teach will be judged with greater strictness. Teachers in the church will be rewarded or suffer loss according to the soundness of their teaching. The Apostle Paul says this about the teachers who followed him to Corinth:

> According to the grace of God given to me, like a skilled master builder I laid a foundation, and someone else is building upon it….Now if anyone builds on the foundation with gold, silver, precious stones, wood, hay, straw - each one's work will become manifest, for the Day will disclose it, because it will be revealed by fire, and the fire will test what sort of work each one has done. If the work that anyone has built on the foundation survives, he will receive a reward. If anyone's work is burned up, he will suffer loss…. *1 Corinthians 3:10-15*

As to those "masters of morals" (see Study Note 1) who judged others and sought to correct them, the words of the Lord apply:

> Judge not, that you be not judged. For with the judgment you pronounce you will be judged, and with the measure you use it will be measured to you. Why do you see the speck that is in your brother's eye, but do not notice the log that is in your own eye? Or how can you say to your brother, 'Let me take the speck out of your eye," when there is a log in your own eye. *Matthew 7:1-4*

2. In what ways may a teacher stumble?

A teacher of the church is in danger of stumbling either in teaching false doctrine or morals, in affirming what he really knows nothing about, or in straying outside his legitimate area of discourse. One example of teaching false doctrine (there are too many to list them all) would be teaching that a good God will not send anyone to hell. An example of someone affirming what he really doesn't know would be identifying the Antichrist, or man of lawlessness, with some figure on the present world stage. An example of teaching outside his legitimate sphere would be opining from the pulpit on the virtues of free enterprise and the vices of socialism, or vice versa.

A "master of morals" is in danger of hypocrisy. Romans 2:17-22, quoted above, gives examples of such hypocrisy. I read only recently of a man heading a Christian work promoting Christian family values who confessed to infidelity in his own family relations. Thanks be to God, he has confessed and is repenting of his sin; but for a time he was a hypocrite. I read later of another man, the pastor of a megachurch, who also confessed to infidelity, but whose subsequent behavior casts doubt on his repentance.

3. James asserts that we all stumble in many ways, especially in our speech. List some ways we stumble and sin in our speech.

A partial list includes boasting, gossip, flattery, false witness, slander, lying, reporting what we really don't know to be true, angry outbursts, hurtful words. No doubt you can think of other ways we sin in speech. Below are a few representative passages of Scripture on the sins of the tongue.

> May the LORD cut off all flattering lips, the tongue that makes great boasts, whose who say, "With our tongue we will prevail, our lips are with us; who is master over us?" *Psalm 12:3-4*

> Let no corrupting talk come out of your mouths, but only such as is good for us, as fits the occasion, that it may give grace to those who hear. *Ephesians 4:29*

> But now you must put them all away: anger, wrath, malice, slander, and obscene talk from your mouth. Do not lie to one another. *Colossians 3:8-9*

4. What is James's point in vs. 4-5, where he uses horses and ships as examples?

The tongue is a small part of the body, but it can do great things. What we say, both to others and to ourselves, can turn the whole man towards one course of action or another, towards good or evil.

5. What is James's main point in vs. 6-10?

James summarized it best in v. 8: "the tongue is a restless evil, full of deadly poison."

6. What is the over-all theme of these verses?

Wisdom, vs. 13, 15, 17.

7. How does one (in particular, a teacher, preacher, or corrector of morals) show himself to be wise? v. 13

He shows his wisdom by his good conduct, doing his works in the meekness that accompanies wisdom. Here, as earlier in the letter, James emphasizes that mere speech without doing the Word, teaching without the works that accompany faith, means nothing.

8. What does meekness mean in the Bible, vs.13-14? Helpful hint: look for the opposite of meekness in these verses; that will help you know what the biblical idea of meekness is.

Biblical meekness is patience, humility, and gentleness. It is the very opposite of frustration and annoyance with those who get in our way, the opposite of self-assertiveness and of harshness with others.

9. Apparently some of those James had in mind boasted about being wise but were not. What showed their so-called wisdom to be unspiritual, earthly, from the devil? v. 16

That so-called wisdom was inspired by jealousy (perhaps of other teachers) and selfish ambition, and resulted in disorder and evil practices.

10. In contrast to unspiritual, devilish "wisdom," what are the hallmarks of divine wisdom from above? v. 17

Purity, peacefulness, gentleness, being open to reason, mercy, a life producing good fruits, impartiality, and sincerity; see 2:1-7.

11. What are the results of wisdom sown (that is, taught or shared) in peace? v. 18

The teaching or sharing of divine wisdom results in a harvest of righteousness. That righteousness consists of the good fruits mentioned in v. 17.

STUDY NOTES

1. Teachers: instructors or moralists?

In 3:1 James introduces a new topic with his characteristic "my brothers." Most commentators believe that the *teachers* to whom he refers are those who preach or instruct the church. John Calvin, however, believed that the Greek word *didaskalos*, usually rendered *teacher* or *master*, was used by James in the sense of one who corrects the morals of others, a "master of morals." Paul used *didaskalos* in this sense:

> But if you call yourself a Jew and rely on the law and boast in God and know his will and approve what is excellent, because you are instructed from the law, and if you are sure that you yourself are a guide to the blind, a light to those who are in darkness, an instructor of the foolish, a teacher [*didaskalon*] of children…you then who teach [*didaskōn*] others, do you not teach yourself? While you preach against stealing, do you steal? You who say that one must not commit adultery, do you commit adultery? You who abhor idols, do you rob temples? *Romans 2:17-22*

It is impossible for us to decide which interpretation of *teachers* James has in mind, preachers and teachers of the whole church or individuals who condemn the behavior and beliefs of others and seek to correct it. However, we have no need to choose an interpretation; James's words apply to both classes of persons.

2. What Scripture teaches about the tongue.

James's teaching about the tongue is in line with the wisdom teaching of the Old Testament. Some representative verses from the Book of Proverbs tell us that the tongue can be used for good or evil.

> The mouth of the righteous is a tree of life, but the mouth of the wicked conceals violence. *10:11*

> The words of the wicked lie in wait for blood, but the mouth of the upright delivers them. *12:6*

> There is one whose rash words are like sword thrusts, but the tongue of the wise brings healing. *12:18*

> A faithful witness does not lie, but a false witness breathes out lies. *14:5*

> Gracious words are like a honeycomb, sweetness to the soul and health to the body. *16:24*

> The words of a whisperer are like delicious morsels; they go down into the inner parts of the body. *18:8*

James implicitly recognizes that words can do good. If they could not, he would tell his hearers that *none* of them should be teachers. But he knows that we sinners are prone to use our tongue for evil rather than good; hence, he emphasizes the dangers of sinful speech over the potential for doing good with our words. Indeed, although the Book of Proverbs commends wise, gracious speech, it also recommends that our words be few lest we sin:

Whoever guards his mouth preserves his life;
he who opens wide his lips comes to ruin. *13:3*

Whoever restrains his words has knowledge,
and he who has a cool spirit is a man of
understanding. Even a fool who keeps silent is
deemed intelligent. *17:27-28*

The tongue cannot be tamed. He who talks too
much is bound to stumble and sin in his speech.
Jesus tells us *why* we are inclined to sin in what we
say:

Either make the tree good and its fruit good, or
make the tree bad and its fruit bad, for the tree
is known by its fruit. You brood of vipers! How
can you speak good, when you are evil? For out
of the abundance of the heart the mouth speaks.
The good person out of his good treasure brings
forth good, and the evil person out of his evil
treasure brings forth evil. I tell you, on the day
of judgment people will give account for every
careless word they speak, for by your words you
will be justified, and by your words you will be
condemned. *Matthew 12:33-37*

3. Verses 13-18: Recognizing true wisdom and its teachers.

James does not begin these verses by addressing
"my brothers," a phrase he often uses to introduce
a new subject. This may indicate that these verses
are a continuation of his warning about becoming
teachers.

Those who teach in the church, as well as those
who presume to tell others their faults and how to
correct them (the "masters of morals"), ought to
be those whose mouths speak wisdom from God.

In these concluding verses of chapter 3 James contrasts true, divine wisdom and earthly, devilish wisdom, and also describes the character of teachers of true wisdom. Not only faith, but faithfulness is shown by one's works.

By applying James's criteria to those who are teaching or correcting them, his hearers will be able to tell which ones to listen to and which to reject. And by applying his criteria to ourselves, whether or not we are teachers we will know how to speak wisely and to sow a harvest of righteousness in peace, v. 18.

4. Meekness: what it is and what it is not.

Most people today don't regard meekness as a desirable character trait. One dictionary defines *meek* as "quiet, gentle, and easily imposed on; submissive." Who wants to be easily imposed on and submissive?

But the Bible speaks highly of meekness. Jesus said in the Sermon on the Mount, "Blessed are the meek, for they shall inherit the earth," Matthew 5:5. In saying this he was quoting Psalm 37:11: "...the meek shall inherit the land." Surely the Bible's concept of meekness is not our modern concept.

James tells us what biblical meekness is; he does so by telling us what it is not. The meek are not jealous or ruled by selfish ambition. Meekness does not seek its own advancement, honor, or advantage. It does not envy those who are successful and covet their achievements or position. It does not have to be first, does not have to have the last word; it does not always have to have its own way.

If we compare James's words with those of the Apostle Paul we see that meek behavior is a form of love

> …love does not envy or boast; it is not arrogant or rude. It does not insist on its own way.
> *1 Corinthians 13:4-7*

James tells us that wisdom is meek. Those who share wisdom with others, either as teachers or as one individual to another, are to do so with patience and gentleness, not with an overbearing, know-it-all attitude, not trying to win the argument through bombast. The Apostle Paul told his protégé Timothy

> …the Lord's servant must not be quarrelsome but kind to everyone, able to teach, patiently enduring evil, correcting his opponents with gentleness. God may perhaps grant them repentance leading to a knowledge of the truth. *2 Timothy 2:24-25.*

5. Recognizing false teachers.

The Apostle Paul describes false teachers in 2 Corinthians 10 and 11:

> Not that we dare to classify or compare ourselves with some of those who are commending themselves. But when they measure themselves by one another and compare themselves with one another, they are without understanding. *10:12*

> Such men are false apostles, deceitful workmen, disguising themselves as apostles of light. *11:13*

He also warns Timothy of such teachers:

The aim of our charge is love that issues from a
pure heart and a good conscience and a sincere
faith. Certain persons, by swerving from these,
have wandered away into vain discussion,
desiring to be teachers of the law, without
understanding either what they are saying or the
things about which they make confident
assertions. *1 Timothy 1:6-7*

For among them [teachers who oppose the
truth] are those who creep into households and
capture weak women, burdened with sins and
led astray by various passions, always learning
and never able to arrive at a knowledge of the
truth….these men also oppose the truth, men
corrupted in mind and disqualified regarding
the faith. *2 Timothy 3:6-8*

LESSON 7. JAMES 4:1-10

STUDY QUESTIONS

1. What is the source of quarrels and fights? *v. 1*

2. We know that quarreling, fighting, and coveting exist among Christians, but *murder*? Can James be writing about Christians here? *v. 2*

3. If there is something we desire, what is the proper course of action? *v. 2*

4. Sometimes we ask but don't receive - why not? *v. 3*

5. Vs.6-10 contain eight imperatives or commands (can you find them all?) Summarize what James is calling for in commanding these things.

ANSWERS TO STUDY QUESTIONS

1. What is the source of quarrels and fights?
v. 1

Quarrels and fights stem from the passions that war within us.

2. We know that quarreling, fighting, and coveting exist among Christians, but murder? Can James be writing about Christians here? v. 2

Possibly. Some Christians then as now were saved from the blackest sins, including murder. Perhaps some might have been tempted to go back to their old ways to get what they wanted.[2] By doing so, of course, they would show by their works that their faith was a dead faith. The Apostle Peter found it necessary to warn Christians against resorting to murder:

> But let none of you suffer as a murderer or a thief or an evildoer or as a meddler. *1 Peter 4:15*

The Apostle John reports these words of God the Father in the Book of Revelation:

> The one who conquers will have this heritage, and I will be his God and he will be my son. But as for the cowardly, the faithless, the detestable, as for *murderers*, the sexually immoral, sorcerers,

---

[2] In the middle of the last century a gangster named Mickey Cohen was supposedly converted by the evangelist Billy Graham. But his lifestyle remained the same. When asked about that, he said, "Christian football players, Christian cowboys, Christian politicians, why not a Christian gangster?"

idolaters, and all liars, their portion will be in the lake that burns with fire and sulfur, which is the second death. *Revelation 21:7-8*, emphasis added.

"The one who conquers" seems to be the Christian who has resisted the temptation to give himself over to the sins that James lists, including murder. It is possible, then, that James has in mind those who claim to be Christian but who actually murder to achieve what they desire.

On the other hand, James may be speaking metaphorically. Consider these words from 1 John:

Everyone who hates his brother is a murderer, and you know that no murderer has eternal life in him. *1 John 3:15*

Jesus taught the same thing in the Sermon on the Mount:

You have heard that it was said to those of old, "You shall not murder; and whoever murders will be liable to judgment." But I say to you, everyone who is angry with his brother will be liable to judgment; whoever insults his brother will be liable to the council; and whoever says, 'You fool!' will be liable to the hell of fire. *Matthew 5:21-22*

It's possible, indeed likely, in this writer's opinion, that James is telling his hearers that their covetous desires which are thwarted by others lead them to hatred which results in quarreling and fighting, and that hatred is murder in the Lord's eyes. That realization should lead to repentance.

Do you hate someone who has what you want or prevents you from getting what you want? Repent of that murder!

3. If there is something we desire, what is the proper course of action? v. 2

We are to ask God for it; but we must ask in faith - recall that if we ask God for wisdom, we must ask in faith, 1:5 - or we cannot expect to receive.

4. Sometimes we ask but don't receive - why not? v. 3

We ask wrongly, only to satisfy our own desires, that is, the desires of the sinful nature.

5. Vs. 6-10 contain eight imperatives or commands (can you find them all?) Summarize what James is calling for in commanding these things.

1. James calls on us twice to *humble ourselves*. The word *humble* occurs twice, once as an adjective, 4:6, and once as a verb, 4:10.

2. He tells us to *submit to God*, 4:7.

3. He implicitly calls for submission when he commands us to *draw near to God*, 4:8.

4. In 4:7 we are called on *to resist the devil*. *To submit* and *to resist* are opposite actions with opposite objects of the action. We submit to God, we resist the devil.

5. Repentance requires *cleansing our hands*, that is, forsaking evil deeds.

6. We are also to *purify our hearts*, forsaking evil desires.

7. James tells us to *mourn and weep over our sins*.

8. Finally, he enjoins us to *abandon the joy we have in the things of the world.*

In summary, James calls for submission to God, resistance to the devil, repentance, and humility. James's admonitions are reminiscent of the Beatitudes, Matthew 5:1-6.

STUDY NOTES

1. A new subject: quarreling and fighting.

The fact that chapter 4 does not begin with "my brothers," words James often uses to indicate a new subject, suggests that what he has to say in 4:1-12 follows on from the end of chapter 3. In 3:13-18 James encouraged meekness, peace, gentleness, being open to reason, mercy, and sincerity. He especially commended peace in 3:18. He now turns his attention to the opposite of peace, quarreling and fighting.

2. The cause of quarreling and fighting: the passions of our old nature.

Quarreling and fighting are, sadly, a feature of Christian life as well as of the world. When we are saved we receive a new nature, but the old nature, sometimes called "the old man" or "the flesh," is not destroyed. Its passions and desires are at war with the desires of our new nature, which are the "desires of the Spirit":

> But I say, walk by the Spirit and you will not gratify the desires of the flesh. For the desires of the flesh are against the Spirit, and the desires of the Spirit are against the flesh, for these are opposed to each other, to keep you from doing the things you want to do....Now the works of the flesh are evident: sexual immorality, impurity, sensuality, idolatry, *sorcery, enmity, strife, jealousy, fits of anger, rivalries, dissensions, divisions, envy,* drunkenness, orgies and things like that. *Galatians 5:16-21a,* emphasis added.

65

Perhaps when we think of the desires of the flesh we think first of sexual desires, drunkenness, and gluttony, but the jealousy, selfish ambition, and disorder of 3:16 and the quarreling and fighting of 4:1 are also works of the flesh, stirred by the desires or passions of the sinful nature.

3. "You ask and you do not receive" - why not?

Jesus' promise that if we ask *anything* in his name he will do it, John 14:13-14, comes with important qualifiers:

a. Jesus will do it so the Father may be glorified in the Son.

> Whatever you ask in my name, this I will do, that the Father may be glorified in the son. If you ask me anything in my name, I will do it. *John 14:13-14*

b. We must abide in him, and his words must abide in us. And, the goal of our prayer must be to bear fruit for God.

> If you abide in me, and my words abide in you, ask whatever you wish, and it will be done for you. By this my Father is glorified, that you bear much fruit and so prove to be my disciples. *John 15:7-8*

How often our prayers are requests for the satisfaction of our own selfish, worldly passions and desires! How seldom are they prayers for the advancement of the kingdom and for God to glorify himself in our lives!

4. Friendship with the world.

James considers our desires and covetousness to be friendship with the world, and he equates friendship with the world with enmity towards God. Indeed, he calls that friendship spiritual adultery in that it amounts to forsaking God, to whom we are pledged, for another. The Bible says that covetousness is idolatry, Ephesians 5:5, and the Old Testament in particular describes idolatry as spiritual adultery, see in particular the Book of Hosea. Hosea 9:1 is a representative verse:

> Rejoice not, O Israel! Exult not like the peoples; for you have played the whore, forsaking your God. You have loved a prostitute's wages on all the threshing floors.

The reason friendship with the world amounts to spiritual adultery is that God demands our entire loyalty and love:

> Hear, O Israel: The LORD our God, the LORD is one. You shall love the LORD your God with all your heart and with all your soul and with all your might. *Deuteronomy 6:4-5*

In v. 5 James tells us that the Scripture says God jealously yearns for our spirit (to be his alone). It is uncertain what passage of Scripture he refers to. He may be alluding indirectly to Genesis 6:3, though he is not quoting the verse - that is only conjecture.

Jesus made it clear that loving the Lord with all our being excludes friendship with the world and all it offers:

No one can serve two masters, for either he will hate the one and love the other, or he will be devoted to the one and despise the other. You cannot serve God and money. *Matthew 6:24*

It is for this reason that James calls for the double-minded to purify their hearts, v. 8.[3] Let us examine our own hearts. If we have divided hearts, we need to purify them by the working of his Spirit and resolve in his grace to be devoted to him alone.

---

[3] Recall that James used the word *doubleminded* in 1:8 to denote those who doubted God. That isn't what it means here. See Lesson 1.

LESSON 8. JAMES 4:11-5:6

STUDY QUESTIONS

1. In 3:9-10 James said that speaking evil of men was sinful because men are made in the image of God. He gives another reason not to speak evil of our brothers or sisters in 4:11. What is it?

2. How does speaking evil against our brother or sister amount to disdaining the law of God? *v.11*

3. What is wrong with the plans of the self-confident people described in v. 13? *vs. 13-16*

4. What must be our attitude towards our future plans? *v. 15*

5. Are the people James addresses in 5:1-6 the same people he has just been dealing with in chapter 4?

6. Are the people James condemns in vs. 1-6 actually Christians?

7. If they are not Christians, why does James address his remarks to them, since his letter was for "the twelve tribes in the dispersion," 1.1?

8. James condemns these people and also warns them. What does he warn them of? *vs. 1-6*

ANSWERS TO STUDY QUESTIONS

1. In 3:9-10 James said that speaking evil of men was sinful because men are made in the image of God. He gives another reason not to speak evil of our brothers and sisters in 4:11. What is it?

Speaking evil against a brother or sister is equivalent to speaking evil against the law of God. We are to *do* the law and not to speak evil of it or judge it. There is only one lawgiver and judge, God. He can save and he can destroy. We endanger our souls by speaking evil against the law, which we do when we speak evil of our brother.

2. How does speaking evil against our brother or sister amount to disdaining the law of God? v. 11

The law tells us to love our neighbor as ourselves. To speak evil against him is to disregard the second great commandment. He who speaks evil against his brother or sister sets the law at naught and invalidates it.

3. What is wrong with the plans of the self-confident people described in v. 13? vs. 13-16

Going to another city to trade is not wrong in itself. Making plans for the future is not wrong; indeed, the Book of Proverbs says it is wise to look ahead and plan ahead:

> Without counsel plans fail, but with many advisers they succeed. *15:22*

Commit your work to the LORD, and your plans will be established. *16:3*

The prudent sees danger and hides himself, but the simple go on and suffer for it. *22:3*

What is wrong with the plans of those James addresses is that no one knows what tomorrow will bring. Failing to recognize this when stating one's plans is boastful arrogance.

Do not boast about tomorrow, for you do not know what a day may bring. *Proverbs 27:1*

It seems that James is alluding to this very verse in James 3:14.

Jesus drove this very point home in the parable of the rich fool, Luke 12:16-21. A rich farmer had stored up many years' worth of grain and goods and decided to take life easy for the rest of his days, which he thought would be many. But God said to him, "Fool! This night your soul is required of you, and the things you have prepared, whose will they be?"[4]

Life is short, and no man knows his time. God is in control of our lives, not we ourselves. Yet the self-assured people James addressed thought they could manage their own destiny.

As a practical matter, do we think and act like them?

4. What must be our attitude towards our future plans? v. 15

We must acknowledge and submissively accept the fact that our pans will only be accomplished if

---

[4] See Ecclesiastes 2:18-1

God so wills.

> The heart of man plans his way, but the LORD establishes his steps *Proverbs 16:9*

We don't necessarily have to add "God willing" as a verbal ending to every expression of what we intend, as Muslims do, but we must add it in our hearts if not on our lips.

5. Are the people James addresses in 5:1-6 the same people he has just been dealing with in chapter 4?

Very likely. Both 4:15 and 5:1 begin with, "Come now," which is at least suggestive that both words of condemnation are addressed to the same people. Also, 5:1 does not begin with "my brothers." In 5:1-6 James addresses the rich; he also seems to be addressing the rich in 4:15-17, though that's not stated explicitly.

6. Are the people whom James condemns in vs. 1-6 actually Christians?

Almost certainly not. The condemnation and judgment they face precludes that. While the reference to murder in 4:2 could be interpreted as a metaphorical reference to hatred, the reference to murder in 5:6 can't so easily be considered *hyperbole*, or exaggeration for the sake of effect.

7. If they are not Christians, why does James address his remarks to them, since his letter was for "the twelve tribes in the dispersion," 1:1?

Although they were not Christians, they may have been church members or adherents (perhaps those who went to church to please a spouse or parent). See Study Note 6.

8. James condemns these people and also warns them. What does he warn them of? vs. 1-6

He warns them of the miseries that will come upon them, v. 1, of the corruption and spoilage of all their wealth, v. 2, of the judgment coming on them for their fraud, v.4, and he warns them that they have fattened themselves in a day of slaughter, v. 5.

STUDY NOTES

1. Who were the judges of the law?

John Calvin believed that James had in mind those "masters of morals" who lorded it over others, criticizing their behavior and telling them how to live (see Lesson 6, Study Note 1). Calvin thought the imposition of one's own moral views on others was what James meant when he said that such persons judge the law when they presume to tell others what the law *really* means, effectively substituting their own ideas of right and wrong for God's commandments. Some contemporary examples of this practice would be condemning a brother or sister for practicing birth control, drinking alcoholic beverages in moderation, not singing psalms exclusively, and voting for the wrong political party. Can you think of more?

2. Speaking evil against a brother: a violation of the law of God.

The Westminster Shorter Catechism interprets the meaning of the ninth commandment, "You shall not bear false witness against your neighbor," broadly. Question 77 asks what is commanded in the ninth commandment. The answer is:

> The ninth commandment requires the maintaining and promoting of truth between man and man, and of our neighbor's good name, especially in witness bearing.

Question 78 asks what is forbidden in the ninth commandment. The answer is:

The ninth commandment forbids whatsoever is prejudicial to truth, or injurious to our own, or our neighbor's good name.

We cannot doubt that the framers of the Shorter Catechism were familiar with James' words.

3. A broad view of the law.

Speaking evil against a brother or sister is also a violation of many of the maxims in the Book of Proverbs. Does the Book of Proverbs give us God's law? When the Bible uses the term *law*, it most often means the Torah, the five books of Moses (Genesis, Exodus, Leviticus, Numbers, and Deuteronomy). But sometimes it has a wider meaning and includes the entire Old Testament. James 1:22-27 suggests that James had the broader meaning of law in mind when he wrote his letter.

Some examples taken from the Book of Proverbs:

Hatred stirs up strife, but love covers all offenses. *10:12*

With his mouth the godless man would destroy his neighbor, but by knowledge the righteous are delivered. *11:9*

Whoever belittles his neighbor lacks sense, but a man of understanding remains silent. Whoever goes about slandering reveals secrets, but he who is trustworthy in spirit keeps a thing covered. *11:12-13*

Whoever covers an offense seeks love, but he who repeats a matter separates close friends. *17:9*

4. The pride of life.

Verses 13-17 should be read with vs. 2, 4, 6, and 8 in mind. James has just written of "friendship with the world," v. 2; coveting, v. 4; pride, v. 6; and being double-minded, that is, trying to love God while loving the world at the same time, v. 8. Those whom he addresses in vs. 13-17 are pursuing the good things of the world with arrogant self-confidence. They are certain they can attain what they seek by their own abilities and talents. They think they are in charge of their own life.

Too many Christians today live the same way. Do you?

5. Knowing versus doing the right thing.

In v. 17 James remind the boasters of vs. 13-16 of the fact that to know the need to submit to God's will and to confess that we are subject to it, and yet not to do it, is sin. This principle has as wide application to us today as to James's original readers. There is much good we know we can and should do. If we fail to do it, we sin. Sins of omission are probably as numerous as sins of commission. We would do well to ask ourselves what good we know we can and should do that we are not doing - and then to be doers of the Word and not hearers only!

6. Does the Bible speak to unbelievers as well as believers?

The Lord told several parables, including the parable of the wheat and the tares and the parable of the net containing both good and bad fish,

Matthew 13, to alert us that in this present age his kingdom or church has both believers and unbelievers in it. It's easy to believe that the churches James knew contained tares as well as wheat.

The pews of churches today are filled with too many who have no saving faith, too many whose life style is as ungodly as those who in James's day kept back the wages of their workers by fraud and lived luxurious lives of self-indulgence. That is why ministers must preach both the gospel and the law of God: they are not just preaching to the choir, even within the walls of a Bible-believing church.

LESSON 9. JAMES 5:7-20

STUDY QUESTIONS

1. In 5:1-6 James warned the wicked that the Last Judgment is coming. How are Christians to view the coming of the Lord? *v. 7*

2. What does it mean to establish our hearts? *v. 8*

3. What encouragement does James offer us to establish our hearts? *v. 8*

4. James wrote his letter 2000 years ago, but the Lord has not yet come. How could he say that the coming of the Lord was "at hand"? *v. 8*

5. In v. 9 James draws another conclusion from the fact that the Judge stands at the door. What is that conclusion?

6. James introduces a new subject in v. 12. What is the subject of this verse?

7. Verse 13 is clear enough, but vs.14 ff. raise questions. Have you ever prayed that God would heal a sick person who was not healed? How can we square that with these verses?

8. What encouragement do you find in vs. 17-18?

9. With what exhortation does James leave us in vs. 19-20?

10. Can a real, born-again Christian wander so far from the truth that his or her soul is in danger of death? *vs. 19-20*

11. The multitude of sins mentioned in verse 20 - whose are they? Those of the wanderer from the truth or those of the brother or sister who brings the sinner back?

ANSWERS TO STUDY QUESTIONS

1. In 5:1-6 James warned the wicked that the Last Judgment is coming. How are Christians to view the coming of the Lord? v. 7

They are to exhibit *patience*, vs. 7, 8, 10, and *steadfastness*, v. 11.

2. What does it mean to establish our hearts? v. 8

To establish our hearts is to fix them on Christ, and not to be shaken by events or lured away by the world.

3. What encouragement does James offer us to establish our hearts? v. 8

The coming of the Lord is at hand.

4. James wrote his letter 2000 years ago, but the Lord has not yet come. How could he say that the coming of the Lord was "at hand"? v. 8

The coming of the Lord was at hand because James and his readers were living in the last days. See Study Note 2.

5. In v. 9 James draws another conclusion from the fact that the Judge stands at the door. What is that conclusion?

We should not grumble against one another. "Grumbling" is just another form of speaking ill of our brothers, and James has twice already condemned and warned against that, 3:9-12 and 4:11-12. Here, where the final judgment is in view, as also in 4:11-12, he warns that God will judge him who speaks ill of his neighbor.

6. James introduces a new subject in v. 12. What is the subject of this verse?

Verse 12 deals with *swearing. Swearing* here does not mean uttering profanity or obscenity, but rather taking an *oath*, that is, "a solemn promise, often invoking a divine witness, regarding one's future action or behavior" (The New Oxford American Dictionary). As the Westminster Confession of Faith puts it,

> the person swearing solemnly calls God to witness what he asserts, or promises, and to judge him according to the truth or falsehood of what he swears. *WCF 22.1*

7. Verse 13 is clear enough, but vs. 14-16 ff. raise questions. Have you ever prayed that God would heal a sick person who was not healed? How can we square that with these verses?

There are several considerations that may bear on a negative answer to a prayer for healing.

a. The sick person is to call for the elders of the church to come and pray and anoint him or her with oil. The prayer that will raise up the sick is a prayer made by the representatives of the church, not simply the prayer of a private believer. To be sure, "the prayer of a righteous person has great power as it is working," v. 16b, whether that righteous person is a pastor, elder or layperson. But the prayer James urges is the prayer of the elders. How often are the elders called in to pray for and to anoint the sick in your church? Let's revive that practice.

b. The prayer may not be made in real faith that God will heal the sick person. James made the point in 1:5-8 that the person who does not pray in faith should not expect to receive anything from the Lord. Sometimes we pray more in desperation than in faith.

c. The sick person is to confess his or her sins, seeking forgiveness as well as healing. When four men brought a paralyzed friend to Jesus to be healed, seeing their faith Jesus said first to the paralytic, "My son, your sins are forgiven," Mark 2:5. Forgiveness is more important than physical healing. If the sick person has no concern for forgiveness, he or she should not expect God to heal.

d. James was writing in the apostolic era, when the Holy Spirit gave miraculous gifts, including the gifts of healing and faith, to some in the church:

> Now there are varieties of gifts, but the same Spirit; and there are varieties of service, but the same Lord; and there are varieties of activities, but it is the same God who empowers them all in everyone. To each is given the manifestation of the Spirit for the common good. To one is given…faith by the same Spirit, to another gifts of healing by the one Spirit, to another the working of miracles. *1 Corinthians 12:4-10*

It doesn't appear that God gives these gifts in the present day. James's words may have been meant for that time and place. Christians should not expect a healing every time we pray for one in our own time.

e. Finally, the statement in v. 15 is not absolute, even though no qualifications are mentioned. The Bible contains many statements that are generally true, but are not true without exception. Some examples follow.

> Whatever you ask in my name, this I will do, that the Father may be glorified in the Son. If you ask me anything in my name, I will do it. *John 14:13-14*

> I have been young, and now am old, yet I have not seen the righteous forsaken, or his children begging bread. *Psalm 37:25*

Three times the Apostle Paul prayed that God would remove his "thorn in the flesh," some kind of physical malady, yet God did not heal him, 2 Cor. 12:7-9.

James himself said, "You ask and do not receive, because you ask wrongly, to spend it on your passions," 4:3.

On one occasion Jesus pointed out to the Pharisees that "you always have the poor with you," Mark 14:7. We cannot assume that they were poor because they were not righteous. The poor woman who cast her last two coins into the temple treasury was commended by Jesus for her generosity.

Finally, consider the following:

> He who finds a wife finds a good thing, and obtains favor from the LORD. *Proverbs 18:22*

Too many men and women, whether divorced or living in an unhappy marriage, would question whether finding a spouse was a good thing for them.

The point of these illustrations is that some statements in Scripture are generally or usually true, but may not be true in all cases, for reasons known to God, and sometimes known to us as well. So it is with the promise of healing.

8. What encouragement do you find in these vs. 17-18?

See 1 Kings 17 and 18 for the story of the great drought that Elijah prayed for at God's command. 1 Kings doesn't tell us of Elijah's prayer or of how long the drought lasted; James gives us that information. But 1 Kings 19, following on the account of the drought, shows us how Elijah was a man just like us, a man of like feelings, as the Greek of James 5:17 puts it. Elijah was not superhuman. He had his fears; he got depressed. But he prayed fervently, in faith, and God answered his prayer. James means to encourage us by citing the example of Elijah. With all our fears and forebodings, we can pray in the confidence that God will answer our prayers.

9. With what exhortation does James leave us in vs. 19-20?

He indirectly urges us to seek out a brother or sister who has wandered from the truth and strive to bring him or her back to the truth.

10. Can a real, born-again Christian wander so far from the truth that his or her soul is in danger of death? (vs. 19-20)

Roman Catholics, Lutherans, and Wesleyans (conservative Methodists, Nazarenes) answer Yes, a Christian can fall away from grace, either by committing a grave (mortal) sin (Roman Catholics and Wesleyans) or by losing their faith (all three groups). Calvinists and dispensationalists answer No. Calvinists believe that God makes his saints persevere in the faith. Dispensationalists put it this way: "once saved, always saved."

What do the Scriptures say?

The Scriptures make it clear that God will keep until the end those he has given to Jesus Christ to be his own people. Jesus said

> And this is the will of him who sent me, that I should lose nothing of all that he has given me but raise it up on the last day. *John 6:39*

Many more Bible passages could be cited to the same effect. What, then, are we to make of James's words?

Scripture sometimes speaks in hypothetical terms with the apparent intention of preventing what it warns against. Jonah preached to the city of Nineveh, "Yet forty days and Nineveh shall be overthrown." The Ninevites repented, and Nineveh was not overthrown. The warning was hypothetical, telling what would happen unless an unmentioned but understood condition, repentance, was met. The warning was meant to prevent the predicted overthrow. So in James, if the wanderer does not return to the truth, he will perish; but the warning is meant to spur *us* on to seek out and bring the wanderer back.

11. The multitude of sins mentioned in v. 20 - whose are they? Those of the wanderer from the truth or those of the brother or sister who brings the sinner back?

They are those of the wanderer from the truth. We cannot cover our own sins by our good deeds. But by bringing the sinner to repentance, God will forgive him or her.

STUDY NOTES

1. Another reason to be patient.

Here James repeats his exhortation to be patient, first raised at the beginning of the letter, 1:2-4. In 5:10 he relates patience to suffering as he did in chapter 1. Here also he connects patience and steadfastness. In the present passage he gives his readers the added encouragement that the coming of the Lord is at hand. That same truth, that the coming of the Lord is at hand, is a warning to the wicked but the "blessed hope" of the Christian, Titus 2:13.

2. When are the last days?

Other New Testament writers also wrote that we are in the last days, even the last hour:

> Long ago, at many times and in many ways, God spoke to our fathers by the prophets, but in these last days he has spoken to us by his Son. *Hebrews 1:1-2*

> But you must remember, beloved, the predictions of the apostles of our Lord Jesus Christ. They said to you, "In the last time there will be scoffers, following their own ungodly passions...." But you, beloved, build yourselves up in your most holy faith...waiting for the mercy of our Lord Jesus Christ that leads to eternal life. *Jude 17-21*

> Children, it is the last hour, and as you have heard that antichrist is coming, so now many antichrists have come. Therefore we know that it is the last hour. *1 John 2:18*

But some 2000 years have passed since the New Testament writers proclaimed that they were living in the last days. How can that be? Even if we are in the last days, were they?

Firstly, we should have no trouble believing that they were living in the last days if we see things from God's perspective.

> For a thousand years in your sight are but as yesterday when it is past, or as a watch in the night. *Psalm 90:4*

The Apostle Peter comments on this verse:

> ...scoffers will come in the last days with scoffing....They will say, "Where is the promise of his coming? For ever since the fathers fell asleep, all things are continuing as they were from the beginning of creation.... But do not overlook this one fact, beloved, that with the Lord one day is as a thousand years and a thousand years as one day. The Lord is not slow to fulfill his promise as some count slowness, but is patient toward you, not wishing that any should perish, but that all should reach repentance. But the day of the Lord will come like a thief, and then the heavens will pass away with a roar, and the heavenly bodies will be burned up and dissolved, and the earth and the works that are done on it will be exposed. *2 Peter 3:3-4, 8-10*

Peter points out that any delay in a second advent that is "at hand" is actually due to God's patience and mercy. He does not bring the present heavens and earth to a fiery conclusion yet because he desires all to come to repentance. It is the longsuffering of God that has prolonged the last days.

3. Should Christians take oaths?

In v. 12 James is restating what Jesus said using some of Jesus's own words:

> Again you have heard that it was said to those of old, "You shall not swear falsely, but shall perform to the Lord what you have sworn." But I say to you, Do not take an oath at all, either by heaven, for it is the throne of God, or by the earth, for it is his footstool, or by Jerusalem, for it is the city of the great King. And do not take an oath by your head, for you cannot make one hair white or black. Let what you say be simply "Yes" or "No"; anything more than this comes from evil. *Matthew 5:33-37*

What James and Jesus say seems pretty clear. Yet we are accustomed to taking oaths in court. Moreover, the Apostle Paul testified with an oath on various occasions:

> For God is my witness…that without ceasing I mention you always in my prayers. *Romans 1:9*

> But I call God to witness against me - it was to spare you that I refrained from coming again to Corinth. *2 Corinthians 1:23*

> As the truth of Christ is in me, this boasting of mine will not be silenced in the regions of Achaia. *2 Corinthians 11:10*

> For we never came with words of flattery, as you know, nor with a pretext for greed - God is witness. *1 Thessalonians 2:5*

Do we disregard the command of James, and of Jesus himself, when we take an oath? The Anabaptists of the early Reformation period, and later the Quakers, answered in the affirmative: we should never swear any oath. John Calvin, the great Reformed theologian, answered in the negative: some oaths are lawful. Calvin's commentary on the Book of James gives his interpretation of this verse.

It has been a common vice almost in all ages, to swear lightly and inconsiderately....For though the Lord strictly commands us to reverence his name, yet men devise various subterfuges, and think they can swear with impunity. They imagine, then, that there is no evil, provided they do not openly mention the name of God....So the Jews, when they swore by heaven or earth, thought that they did not profane God's name because they did not mention it....

It was a vain excuse of this kind that Christ condemned in Matthew 5:34. James, now subscribing to the decree of his master, commands us to abstain from these indirect forms of swearing; for whosoever swears in vain and on frivolous occasions, profanes God's name, whatever form he may give to his words....

James does not speak of oaths in general, nor does Christ in the passage to which I have referred; but both condemn that evasion which had been devised, when men took the liberty to swear without expressing the name of God....Now James condemns those who did not indeed dare in a direct way to profane God's name, but endeavored to evade the profanation which the law condemns, by circumlocutions.

Calvin's interpretation, which has been accepted by the Reformed and Presbyterian churches, is based on an assumption which is not found in the biblical text. That doesn't mean that it's incorrect; possibly Calvin deemed the example of the Apostle Paul to be indirect evidence that Christians may swear by God himself.

I suggest we apply to this question the Apostle Paul's words, written with another debatable issue in mind:

Each one should be fully convinced in his own mind. *Romans 14:5*

PUBLISHER'S INFORMATION

This book is part of the Timothy Series of study guides published by Saluda Press, Tacoma, WA. Go to the Saluda Press website, www.saludapress.com, to buy copies of this study guide and other study guides in the series. If you have questions or comments, email publisher@saludapress.com.